Animals
in the
Stars

Chinese Astrology
for Children

Written & Illustrated by
Gregory Crawford

Bear Cub Books
Rochester, Vermont

Dedicated to the memory of Christopher Robin Densmore

Bear Cub Books
One Park Street
Rochester, Vermont 05767
www.InnerTraditions.com

Bear Cub Books is a division of Inner Traditions International

Library of Congress Cataloging-in-Publication Data
Crawford, Gregory.
   Animals in the stars : Chinese astrology for children / written and illustrated by Gregory Crawford.
      p. cm.
   Summary: Includes an overview of the history of the Chinese zodiac (The Twelve Earthly Branches,) a birth-year chart, and twelve folktales, each featuring one of the animals.
   ISBN 978-1-59143-000-1
   1. Astrology, Chinese—Juvenile literature. 2. Animals—Folklore—Juvenile literature.   [1. Astrology, Chinese. 2. Zodiac. 3. Animals—Folklore. 4. Folklore—China.]   I. Title.
   BF1714.C5C75 2003
   133.5'9251—dc21

   2002009984

Printed and bound in India by Replika Press Pvt Ltd.

10 9 8 7 6 5 4 3

Text design and layout by Cynthia Ryan Coad
This book was typeset in Stone Informal and Stone Sans

Contents

The Story of the Twelve Earthly Branches

A long time ago, when the world was very young, there was a beautiful land called Zhonngguo, which means the Middle Kingdom. To this very day the people who live there call it by this name, but we call it China.

The people of this enchanted land were very wise and closely watched the world around them. They observed the trees blossoming in the spring and shedding their leaves in the fall. They noticed the world as it grew green in the summer and as it dreamed under a blanket of snow in the winter. They watched the animals, both male and female, as they went about their lives through every season, and they looked up at the skies above—at the Sun and Moon. In this way the people of the Middle Kingdom learned how to live in harmony with nature and its opposites of *yin,* or female energy, and *yang,* male energy. In fact, this way of living became so important to many of them that they gave it a name: Taoism (pronounced "Dowism").

Some of those who studied this way of living and followed it closely each day became knowledgeable and wise priests. They could feel in the wind when the rains would come, and they could predict how great the harvest would be. But neither they nor the people of Zhonngguo had a way of marking and dividing time, as we do

today with our calendar. And strangely enough, they did not always understand each other as well as they understood the animals around them.

How did they come to be able to mark time and understand their neighbors and friends? Here is how one story tells it.

Some of the priests who lived in the Middle Kingdom were quite old; they had lived through many years. And as they looked back on their lives and thought about all that had happened in Zhonngguo, they began to see that some years were full of slow-but-steady effort and patient strength, as though the strong and steady Ox were in charge. Other years seemed full of courageous deeds and daring, just like powerful Tiger. Some were years of action and success, as though Monkey ruled over all, while others were time for careful thought and planning, as though guided by Snake. After talking to one another and closely watching the animals around them, they discovered that each year they could recall seemed to be influenced by one of twelve different animals: Ox, Tiger, Monkey, Snake, Rat, Boar, Rabbit, Dog, Horse, Rooster, Sheep, and (whether real or not!) the important Dragon.

"Aha!" the priests said to one another. This meant to them that all time was governed by a repeating cycle of twelve years ruled by these twelve animals, an Ox year followed by a Tiger year, followed by a Rabbit year, and so on until all twelve years had gone by and the Ox year came around again—much like time for us is governed by a repeating cycle of twelve months, January followed by February followed by March, and so on, until all twelve months have gone by and January comes around again. The priests called this cycle of twelve years the Twelve Earthly Branches—which today we call the Chinese zodiac.

But their discoveries didn't stop there. Not only years were influenced by these twelve animals. All the people they observed seemed to be ruled by them too! Those born in a year ruled by Rooster, a year of hard work and discipline, were, sure enough, the hardest working, most disciplined people in the Middle Kingdom. And those born in a peaceful and happy Sheep year were the calmest and most content people anyone knew.

The priests had discovered a way of both dividing time and understanding people—all in all, an amazing feat for which Huang Ti, the Jade Emperor, praised them greatly. "But," the emperor asked them, "if we are to use this system to help us mark time, we must know which year begins the cycle. You must decide which animal comes first."

How It Was Decided Which Animal Came First

The priests debated the issue for a long time, with each one arguing that his birth year and guiding animal should have the honor of beginning the cycle. Finally, one priest said something wise and sensible: "But we can't all be first! Let's ask the emperor himself to decide!"

When they appeared before the Jade Emperor, the priests bowed and the eldest one said, "Your Highness, we believe only you, in your infinite wisdom, could decide which animal should come first in the cycle of the Twelve Earthly Branches."

"Very well," said the emperor, "but I must spend some time considering this." With that, the priests left the emperor to his thoughts.

After a great deal of pondering, he finally arrived at a solution. The emperor summoned a court scribe and instructed him to send out invitations to each of the twelve animals, requesting that they join the Jade Emperor for a great feast. Soon messengers began combing the countryside to deliver the invitations.

Dog, lying in the shade and guarding her master's home, wagged her tail excitedly when her invitation arrived. Ox, standing in a rice paddy and chewing her cud, kicked up her hooves with glee. When Tiger received the emperor's request, he roared his delight; and when Monkey opened her invitation, she ran up a tree. Rooster crowed that he would be honored to attend, and Rabbit scampered back into her thicket to pack. Boar rooted in the mud for a suitable gift, and Rat hid one last armload of grain before she set out on her journey to the palace. Horse trotted out his finest halter for the occasion, while Sheep shook the dust from his wool. Snake shed his old skin so he might appear glossy and bright, and Dragon considered bringing some fireworks but then thought better of it.

And so it was that twelve animals set out from every corner of the Middle Kingdom to the palace of the Jade Emperor. Some had considerable distances to travel, but they all shared a steadfast determination to be the first to arrive and honor their ruler.

Rat was resting to catch her breath after climbing a steep hill when her old friend, Ox, trudged up the road toward her. Rat called out to Ox with great self-importance, "Hello, Ox! I have been invited to dine with the Jade Emperor this evening!"

Ox raised her eyebrows appreciatively and nodded. Being an ox of few words, she simply said, in her deep rumbling voice, "And so have I."

Rat thought about this, looked at the palace, tiny in the distance, and then gazed ahead of them at the long road that turned and wove between fields of rice on its meandering way. A plan was forming in Rat's mind and she said, "Ox, my old friend, see how the road wanders through the countryside? It seems to me that we could save a lot of time by going in a straight line right across all those rice fields. With your great size and strength it would be a simple journey."

5

Ox quickly saw the truth of this and the two animals set off together down the hill. But when they reached the edge of the first rice paddy, Rat gingerly dipped a toe in the muddy water and, looking at Ox from the corner of her eye, said mournfully, "I suppose I shall have to brave it, dear Ox, no matter how dangerous it may be for me!"

Ox, always thinking of the troubles of others, said, "Nonsense, Rat! The water is far too deep for you. Climb onto my back and I will carry you across the field. You can keep us going in the right direction."

Rat's plan had worked! She thanked Ox and leaped onto her broad back. And so it was that Rat kept them on course as Ox plowed through the underbrush and the rice paddies until their cooperation brought them to the gates of the palace well ahead of the other animals. The guards led them to the doors of the emperor's great hall.

Both animals gazed in awe at the silks and marble and finery in the huge room—and in a moment they saw the Jade Emperor himself! Rat froze, overwhelmed by the ruler's grandeur, but then remembered to inch herself a few steps beyond Ox so that the emperor might see her first as she bowed low to the floor.

"Welcome, Rat!" the emperor said with a smile. "And welcome to you, too, Ox! Rat, you have honored me by being the first guest to arrive, and so you shall be honored by being the first animal in the cycle of the Twelve Earthly Branches! And you, Ox, shall be second!"

And that is how it came to be that the Year of the Rat begins the twelve-year cycle of the Chinese zodiac.

Finding Your Animal Year

If you know the year when you were born, then you can use the chart on page 7 to learn which animal influences you—and if you know the birth years of your friends, you can find their ruling animals too. Remember, because the Chinese zodiac is a cycle that repeats over and over like the months of our year, people of all ages will share your animal year—which means you can hunt for your parents' or teachers' animals too!

To use the chart, in the column on the right find the year when you were born. Then look to the column on the left to find your animal. Next, turn to your animal in the following pages to read about the characteristics and personality traits that you and all who share your animal may have.

On the page next to each description you'll find a story drawn from a traditional Chinese folktale featuring your animal. The animals of Chinese astrology—even the mythical dragon—were chosen in part because they figured closely in the everyday life of ancient China. Telling folktales was one way to teach values and to entertain and many of them used these same animals as characters because everyone was so familiar with them.

Today we may not be as familiar with all of the qualities of the twelve animals in the Chinese zodiac. In fact, we may think of some of them a bit differently than the ancient Chinese did (some of us may not have a very good impression of Snake, for instance). The following pages, then, may help you learn to see some animals—and maybe even yourself!—in a new and different way.

Chinese Zodiac

Animal	Year of Birth		Animal	Year of Birth		Animal	Year of Birth		Animal	Year of Birth		Animal	Year of Birth	
Rat	1924	1984	Rat	1936	1996	Rat	1948	2008	Rat	1960	2020	Rat	1972	2032
Ox	1925	1985	Ox	1937	1997	Ox	1949	2009	Ox	1961	2021	Ox	1973	2033
Tiger	1926	1986	Tiger	1938	1998	Tiger	1950	2010	Tiger	1062	2022	Tiger	1974	2034
Rabbit	1927	1987	Rabbit	1939	1999	Rabbit	1951	2011	Rabbit	1963	2023	Rabbit	1975	2035
Dragon	1928	1988	Dragon	1940	2000	Dragon	1952	2012	Dragon	1964	2024	Dragon	1976	2036
Snake	1929	1989	Snake	1941	2001	Snake	1953	2013	Snake	1965	2025	Snake	1977	2037
Horse	1930	1990	Horse	1942	2002	Horse	1954	2014	Horse	1966	2026	Horse	1978	2038
Sheep	1931	1991	Sheep	1943	2003	Sheep	1955	2015	Sheep	1967	2027	Sheep	1979	2039
Monkey	1932	1992	Monkey	1944	2004	Monkey	1956	2016	Monkey	1968	2028	Monkey	1980	2040
Rooster	1933	1993	Rooster	1945	2005	Rooster	1957	2017	Rooster	1969	2029	Rooster	1981	2041
Dog	1934	1994	Dog	1946	2006	Dog	1958	2018	Dog	1970	2030	Dog	1982	2042
Boar	1935	1995	Boar	1947	2007	Boar	1959	2019	Boar	1971	2031	Boar	1983	2043

1900 · 1912 · 1924
1936 · 1948 · 1960
1972 · 1984 · 1996

鼠 The Year of the Rat

The Year of the Rat is a time of prosperity, abundance, and good fortune for all. It is a year marked by small but steady gains, like those a busy rat might experience when she builds her winter store of food a little bit at a time until her burrow is full.

The rat is disliked in most Western cultures—just think of what we call someone who's disloyal, sneaky, or a tattletale ("You dirty rat!"). But in Asia she's seen a little differently. The rat does have a reputation as a devious trickster, but she's still held in high regard for her cleverness in finding and keeping her wealth.

A person born in the Year of the Rat . . .

- Is intelligent—though it may not always show in her grades at school.
- Is a hard worker who sticks to the job no matter what.
- Is willing to sacrifice a great deal to achieve the things she wants.
- Is patient and generous to loved ones.
- Is a charmer—a funny "people person."

But Rat can have trouble if . . .

- She works and sacrifices too much—others may see this as greediness and selfishness.
- She lets her suspicious nature take control.

Friends and Others . . .

- Rat might not get along with: Horse
- Rat's best companions: Ox, Dragon, and Monkey

Rat's Big Day at the Market

Rat and Ox were good friends, but Rat was a devilish little prankster—and she was bored. So she began to tease her friend.

"Poor Ox! How jealous you must be that I am so very much bigger than you!"

Now, Ox should have known better than to be drawn in by mischievous Rat, but instead she snorted and replied, "Of course you're not bigger than I am, Rat! How could I be jealous of you? Everyone knows that I am one hundred times your size!"

Rat sprang to her feet (the bait had been taken!): "*Everyone* knows, Ox? Well, we certainly can't ask *everyone* which of us is bigger—so let the crowd at the market decide! I'll even let you go first so they can see just how big you really are! Whoever attracts the most attention for her size alone shall win the debate!"

Ox simply shook her great head in exasperation, thinking, "Fool of a Rat!" but she smiled and agreed to these terms.

In the street she marched slowly and grandly with her nose in the air so everyone at the market might see what a really big ox she was. But no one paid her the least bit of attention; after all, people saw oxen every day.

Rat, in the meantime, proceeded to gorge herself on everything in sight. She funneled fistfuls of grain into her mouth, gnawed on nuts, and guzzled a gallon of water in just a few minutes until her belly was swollen to twice its normal size and she could barely waddle to the market. But waddle she did, and the moment Rat plopped herself down in front of everyone, Ox knew she'd been had. A great murmur rippled through the crowd, "Did you see the size of that rat?" "Biggest rat I ever saw!" "Now *that's* a big rat! Boy, you don't see many rats like that anymore!"

Everyone in the market gathered to marvel at Rat's size. They threw coins and food to her while she paraded about with her nose in the air, smiling with delight and winking at Ox, who simply shook her great head in exasperation at being taken in once again.

1901 · 1913 · 1925
1937 · 1949 · 1961
1973 · 1985 · 1997

牛 The Year of the Ox

The Year of the Ox is a time in which problems are solved through patience, determination, and strength. "Slow but steady" is the rule for this year.

The musk ox has been such an important part of Chinese life since ancient times that she is found in sculptures, paintings, songs, and stories going back to the beginning of Chinese history.

A person born in the Year of the Ox . . .

- Is calm and gentle and incredibly strong.
- Thinks through problems completely, no matter how long it takes, before deciding what to do.
- Will not give up working until a problem is solved or a job is done.
- Is a great listener and doesn't speak unless she has something important to say.
- Is a helpful, solid, and reliable friend who offers good advice.

But Ox can have trouble if . . .

- She's prodded a little too much. It's hard to stir Ox's anger, but once she's angry, she's ANGRY!
- She doesn't reach her goal, which can make her very upset.
- Someone tries to give her advice—she can be quite stubborn!

Friends and Others . . .

- Ox might not get along with: Sheep, Horse, or Dog
- Ox's best companions: Snake, Rooster, and Rat—and another Ox makes a good friend too

10

How the Ox Learned Patience

Long ago, when the world was still new, life was quite hard and people seldom had enough to eat. They gathered roots and berries and hunted when they could, but they often went hungry for days. The Emperor of the Sky saw the people scrabbling in the dirt, looking for anything they might eat, and he felt sorry for them. Turning his eyes to the vast night sky above him, he saw the Ox star and beckoned to his loyal subject.

"Ox," proclaimed the emperor, "I want you to go down and tell the people of the earth to gather as many of their favorite grains and vegetables as they can find in this lean time. Then tell them to plow the ground and plant them in a place where they can tend them. The few vegetables and grains they are able to collect will produce many seeds that can be planted in the spring, and in this way they will have food enough at least to enjoy a meal every three days. Now repeat my instructions."

But Ox was eager to help the people and couldn't wait a moment longer. "Don't worry, I'll remember!" she called as she hurriedly marched toward earth to deliver the emperor's message.

When she arrived, she was so overcome by the sad state of the people that she couldn't wait to share her news of relief: "People of the earth, the Emperor of the Sky bids me tell you to gather as many of your favorite grains and vegetables as you are able to find, then plow the earth and plant them in one place where you can tend them. If you save the seeds that these produce and plant them in the spring, you will have enough food to enjoy three meals every day!"

The people began to talk among themselves about the Ox's message, but no sooner did she finish speaking than she turned and headed back to her home, so eager to tell the emperor how successful her mission had been that she couldn't wait to hear what the people had to say.

After hearing what Ox had said on earth, the emperor bellowed, "Ox, you ninny! I said they'd enjoy 'a meal every three days,' not 'three meals every day!' The people of earth are scrawny things with spindly legs that are weakened from hunger! They can't possibly plow enough earth to plant all they need for three meals a day!"

Ox bowed her head in shame. "A thousand pardons, your majesty!" she said, and then hoping to repair her mistake as quickly as she could without waiting another minute, she added, "I'll go right down and tell them of my error and then I'll come right back and—"

"Ox, you made a promise to the people in my name. Now you must see that it is honored."

Eager to please both the emperor and the people, Ox nodded her head vigorously and turned to gallop toward the earth. But behind her the emperor's voice spoke once again: "And Ox—it's high time you slowed down and learned a little patience!"

And so Ox left her place as a star in the sky and returned to earth, where she used her great strength to pull a plow all day long, very slowly and very patiently.

1902 · 1914 · 1926
1938 · 1950 · 1962
1974 · 1986 · 1998

虎 The Year of the Tiger

The Year of the Tiger is a time for daring and courageous deeds, an exciting time of bold creativity. It is a year of extremes when things happen in a way that can seem bigger than life.

In Chinese mythology tigers guard the four points of the compass—north is guarded by the black tiger, south by the red tiger, east by the green tiger, and west by the white tiger.

A person born in the Year of the Tiger . . .

- Is a strong and magnetic natural leader, with courage and passion for solving problems.
- Is a shy and sensitive loner—like the king in a fairy tale who can't ever share his sadness or fears because those around him might think he's cowardly or timid.
- Never follows the crowd—Tiger prefers to be independent.
- Keeps his word, no matter what.
- Sets high expectations for himself and others.

But Tiger can have trouble if . . .

- He does something because he thinks he's following his independent streak but is really only trying to do the opposite of what he's *supposed* to do.
- His courage and passion and independence make him leap before he looks!

Friends and Others . . .

- Tiger might not get along with: Snake or Monkey
- Tiger's best companions: Horse, Dragon, and Dog

Tiger Makes a Promise

One day Mouse was scampering through the forest, too intent on getting home, when he bumped right into Tiger's nose and suddenly found himself surrounded by the great cat's huge paws. Tiger smiled down with a glint in his amber eyes and asked lazily, "And just where might you be going in such a hurry, Mouse?"

Mouse knew that he was in trouble. Bowing low and quivering with fear, he pleaded with commanding Tiger, "Oh, most noble sir, I was hurrying home to my family! I beg of you, please, do not eat me! I am too tiny a morsel for one so great and strong! My family depends on me and they would suffer untold misery if I were to end up as a mere snack for the king of the forest."

Tiger was not especially hungry at the moment and he rather liked being bowed to and pleaded with, so he chose to be generous. "Fear not little Mouse, I'll spare you . . . today!" Mouse flinched as Tiger smiled. "Run along home to your family—and watch where you're going next time!"

Mouse scurried down the path a little way, then turned and said to Tiger, "Thank you, sir, for sparing my life. May your kindness be repaid with a future of good fortune!" With that, Mouse disappeared into the bushes and Tiger resumed his nap.

A few days later, while padding silently along a favorite path, Tiger stepped into a net snare hidden in the leaves on the forest floor and soon found himself dangling upside down a few feet off the ground. As he struggled in vain to free himself, Mouse came down the same path, watching out for tigers all the while. He soon spotted the king of the forest in his humiliating predicament and, after thinking a moment, quickly vanished into the undergrowth.

Tiger roared in anger and despair until Mouse returned moments later with his entire family—and a few cousins. "Fear not, Tiger, we'll have you free shortly!" The mice quickly gnawed through the ropes that held Tiger captive, and, just as promised, Mouse and his family set Tiger free.

In his gratitude, Tiger made a promise in return—never to eat or frighten another mouse for the rest of his life. And he kept his word.

1903 · 1915 · 1927
1939 · 1951 · 1963
1975 · 1987 · 1999

兔 The Year of the Rabbit

The Year of the Rabbit is calm, peaceful, and uneventful—time for us to catch our breath, think back, and look ahead after a tumultuous year ruled by Tiger.

In China the rabbit has long been associated with the moon and good luck and people believed that good fortune would follow if the first words they composed in the new year were written with a brush made of fine rabbit hair.

A person born in the Year of the Rabbit . . .

- **Is gentle, friendly, caring—and quite romantic.**
- **Prefers being with people and dislikes being alone for any length of time.**
- **Is very sensitive and is very troubled by arguments or conflict of any kind.**
- **Can't bear to make enemies and tries hard to avoid saying or doing anything that might hurt someone's feelings.**
- **Is creative and loves things that are pleasing to the eye.**

But Rabbit can have trouble if . . .

- **She gives in to spending too much time on style and beauty!**
- **She gives in to her love of gossip—which may mean that someone's feelings will be hurt!**

Friends and Others . . .

- **Rabbit might not get along with: Dragon, Rat, or Rooster**
- **Rabbit's best companions: Sheep, Dog, and Boar**

14

The Rabbit in the Moon

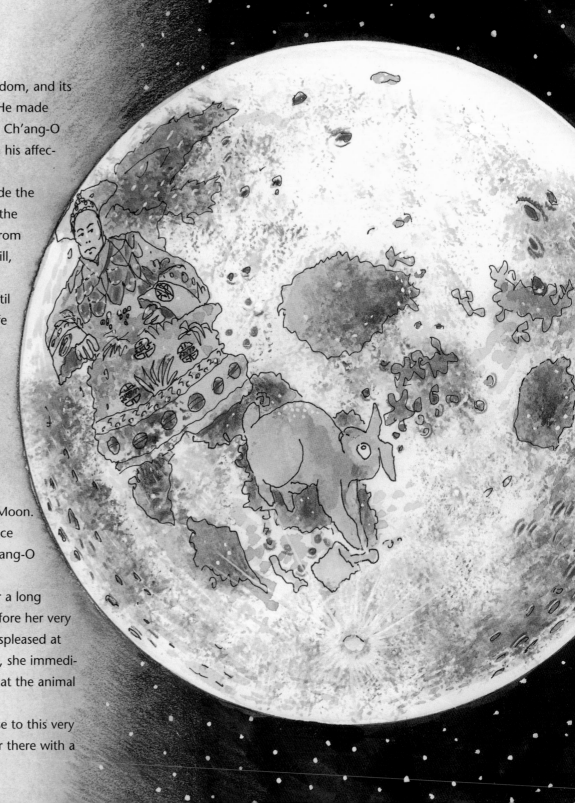

Long ago, in a remote corner of China, there was a small, rustic kingdom, and its ruler, Ho-Yi, fell in love with Ch'ang-O, the prettiest girl in the land. He made her his wife and showered her with jewels and finery, but the spoiled Ch'ang-O found the king's rough country manners repulsive and did not return his affection, no matter how generous his gifts were.

On the birthday and festival of the Queen of the Skies, Ho-Yi made the long journey to honor her and offer his best wishes. In appreciation, the Queen of the Skies gave Ho-Yi a pill containing a magic elixir made from the fur of a divine white rabbit who was a thousand years old. This pill, she said, would make him live forever!

Ho-Yi was exhausted upon returning from his trip. "I can wait until tomorrow to live forever," he said to himself, and, after telling his wife his story, he entrusted the pill to her and then fell asleep.

Ch'ang-O, however, remained wide awake. Fascinated by the story of the pill's power, she decided to eat it—and found that she could fly!

In the morning Ho-Yi was furious to learn of his wife's treachery, but before he could punish her, she flew off to hide in a cave on the moon. Ho-Yi pursued her but was turned away by Wu-Kang, the guardian of the Skies.

The Queen of the Skies then appointed Ch'ang-O Queen of the Moon. This made Ho-Yi furious. In his anger and frustration, he turned his face toward the darkened night sky and yelled at the moon. He knew Ch'ang-O could hear him, for he heard the taunts she screamed back at him.

From the mouth of her cave on the moon, Ch'ang-O hollered for a long time—until, with one great holler, she coughed up the magic pill. Before her very eyes it turned back into a white rabbit! Spoiled Ch'ang-O was *very* displeased at losing the pill, and, afraid that she would lose her immortality as well, she immediately thrust a mortar and pestle into the rabbit's paws, demanding that the animal make another pill for her.

The poor rabbit, however, must have forgotten the recipe because to this very day, if you look at the full moon in just the right way, you can see her there with a mortar and pestle, beside the Queen of the Moon, Ch'ang-O.

1904 · 1916 · 1928
1940 · 1952 · 1964
1976 · 1988 · 2000

龍 *The Year of the Dragon*

The Year of the Dragon is a time of power and ambition. Everything that happens seems bigger than life and much more exciting. It is the year to take giant steps forward.

In Chinese mythology dragons were important symbols of royalty and wisdom. In fact, the emperors of China wore the dragon robe and sat upon the dragon throne.

A person born in the year of the Dragon . . .

- Has been given four special blessings by the gods: harmony, virtue, prosperity, and long life.
- Is brave and adventurous—and never gives up.
- Is independent, creative, and full of feeling.
- Dreams of making great changes in the world.

But Dragon can have trouble if . . .

- He can't focus his energy on changing the world—Dragon isn't much interested in life's daily chores and can be quite lazy about getting them done!
- His sensitive feelings are stirred up or hurt. (This can make him "leap" before he "looks!")
- He's surrounded by uppity or snooty behavior—he has very little patience for snobbishness!

Friends and Others . . .

- Dragon might not get along with: Ox, Rabbit, Dog—and another Dragon
- Dragon's best companions: Monkey, Rat, Snake, and Rooster

The Golden Dragon

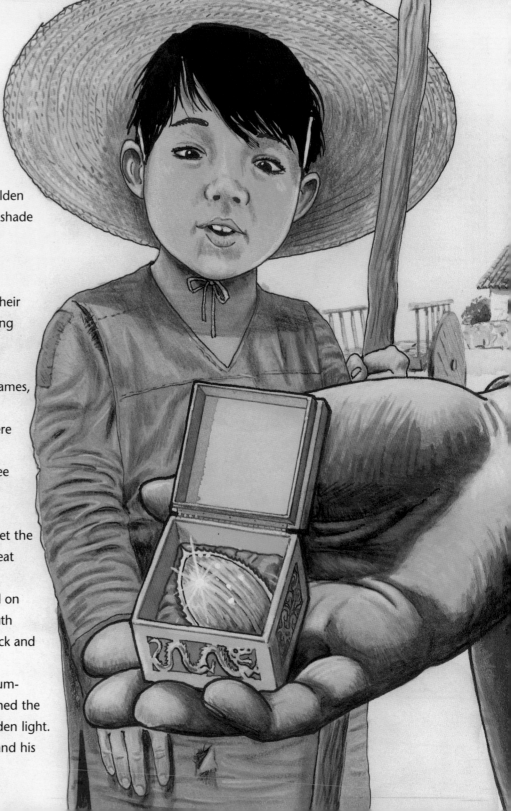

Many years ago, a quiet, thoughtful boy named Wu often stood at the gate of his father's farm to watch the world beyond. One day, he watched as a small party made its way toward him. As they drew closer, Wu could see it was led by a handsome young man in golden robes riding a fine white horse whose glistening coat seemed, each moment, to change color in the sunlight.

When the procession approached the gate, the noble young man in the golden robes said, "Wu, son of Yin, I am tired and thirsty. May I rest awhile in the cool shade of your father's courtyard?"

The boy, feeling very honored, bowed and replied, "Please enter."

Wu's father, Yin, happily welcomed the visitors with food and drink.

When the noble young man was rested, he thanked Wu and his father for their hospitality, and as he and his company passed through the gate, the noble young man said to the boy, "I shall return tomorrow."

Wu bowed solemnly and responded, "Please come."

When the guests were out of sight, Wu's father whispered, "He knew our names, but we've never seen him before!"

Wu, whose eyes were sharp from watching the world, said, "Their robes were seamless! The horse's body was covered with colored scales instead of hair, and neither his hooves nor their feet touched the ground as they walked! Did you see them just now? They rose into the air and disappeared into those rain clouds."

Yin exclaimed, "They must be spirits!"

When they told Wu's aged grandmother of the visitors, she agreed. "You met the Golden Dragon and his dragon horse." She cautioned then, "He will bring a great storm!"

And so he did. A terrible storm swept away the whole village—but no rain fell on Wu's home. When the skies cleared and the flood waters receded, the golden youth returned. He handed Wu a small box containing a single scale from his horse's neck and said, "Keep this and I shall remember you."

Soon the emperor heard of the flood and the miracle of Wu's survival. He summoned Wu and his father to tell him the story. Upon finishing the tale, Wu opened the box and the single dragon scale illuminated the entire room with a brilliant golden light.

Wu's story and the scale won him great respect from the emperor, and he and his family lived in comfort to the end of their days.

1905 · 1917 · 1929
1941 · 1953 · 1965
1977 · 1989 · 2001

虫它 The Year of the Snake

The Year of the Snake is a time to look inside ourselves and plan for the future. Careful thought will guide your actions, and good taste and elegance will be the rule. The wisdom of Snake will smooth any disasters or difficulties left over from the Dragon year that has just passed.

Since ancient times the snake has been associated with the sun. Because he sheds his skin, the snake has come to symbolize rebirth and renewal, like the rising of the sun that marks a new day.

A person born in the Year of the Snake . . .
- **Has plenty of creativity and stylish flair.**
- **Is friendly and outgoing—but rarely reveals his deepest thoughts and feelings.**
- **Is charming in a crowd, but would just as soon be home alone with a good book as be out at a party.**
- **Is very perceptive and smart.**
- **Thinks deeply and questions everything.**
- **Makes quick decisions to solve a problem.**

But Snake can have trouble if . . .
- **Keeping his thoughts and feelings to himself causes other people to see him as aloof or secretive.**
- **His insecurity and deep thoughts cause him to be jealous.**

Friends and Others . . .
- **Snake might not get along with: Tiger or Boar**
- **Snake's best companions: Ox and Rooster**

The Snake, the Deer, and the Old Man

After months of rain the river Dedong overflowed its banks and flooded the valleys of Pyongyang as it never had before. A poor and ragged old man rowed his weathered boat through the flood waters, trying to get to safety.

As he rowed, he spied an exhausted deer struggling against the strong current. The old man managed to pull the animal to the safety of his boat. Before long, he came upon a boy calling for help. The old man stretched his oar to the youth and, once he was safely aboard, warmed him with his only blanket. Soon after, the man spotted a snake, helpless in the swift water. He scooped him up and set him under his seat to rest.

When the four reached dry land, the old man stroked the deer's neck and wished her well before she bounded off into the forest. Then he caressed the snake's smooth skin and placed him on a sunny rock out of harm's way. The boy, however, had lost his family, so the kind old man fed him and adopted him as his own son.

Time passed and one day the old man saw the deer again. She bounded toward him and tugged at his sleeve until he followed her to a hidden glen. There she pawed the ground and then looked at him. The man began to dig—and soon found a chest full of gold!

He was wealthy—a pauper no more! But the old man's adopted son squandered money foolishly and rudely ignored his father's warnings to curb his spending. Finally, the old man was forced to cut off the boy's allowance. In return, the selfish youth told the police that the old man claimed his riches were the gift of the deer. He knew the police would find the story suspicious and jail the old man—which is exactly what happened.

But one night, while the old man dozed in his jail cell, a snake slithered through the bars, bit him, and disappeared. As the old man's arm began to swell painfully, the snake returned with a small vial in his mouth. The man poured one drop on his wound and, to his amazement, the pain ceased.

The next morning, the guard told him that the magistrate's wife had been bitten by a snake and lay dying. The old man said that he might be able to help. At the woman's bedside, he murmured some prayers and poured a drop from the vial onto her wound. In no time at all, the swelling disappeared and the woman opened her eyes and smiled at him.

The magistrate released the old man with warm gratitude—and hearing this, the selfish boy left the valleys of Pyongyang, where the old man lived the rest of his days in peace.

1906 · 1918 · 1930
1942 · 1954 · 1966
1978 · 1990 · 2002

馬 The Year of the Horse

The Year of the Horse is a time of adventure, excitement, and romance, a time when decisive action and high energy can bring success. But it's also a time of extremes; things can go very well, or they can go very badly!

A person born in the Year of the Horse . . .

- Is bright, cheerful, and fun-loving.
- Loves companionship and is usually surrounded by friends.
- Will always tell you the truth and exactly what's on his mind.
- Is like Boar in his love of things that are beautiful and extravagant — lovely clothes, delicious food, and music, music, and more music!
- Is very good at making decisions.

But Horse can have trouble if . . .

- He meets someone who is sneaky (he doesn't like anyone who isn't honest) or wishy-washy (he isn't always patient with those who can't make decisions).
- He spends a little too much money on extravagant things.
- He doesn't always have fun while learning something new, such as how to play basketball or the piano, for instance—Horse can give up on something too soon, even if others are counting on him.

Friends and Others . . .

- Horse might not get along with: Ox, Rabbit, or another Horse—and Rat, his exact opposite
- Horse's best companions: Tiger, Dog, and Sheep

The Horse Who Knew the Way

The horse Kao Ma had carried Huo-hsin since both he and Huo-hsin were young. They had survived many battles over the years because they trusted and understood each other. They communicated in that way known only to horses and people who have shared much.

Kao Ma could tell, then, that his friend was worried. Huo-hsin and the rest of the army of Chi were following General Huang-hua, the man who had deserted the invaders from Ku-Chu and joined their side in the fight. The general had led them all into the desert, where the wind blew constantly and the drifting sands erased Kao Ma's tracks as soon as he lifted his feet.

As they walked, Kao Ma asked his friend, "Huo-hsin, why do we wander aimlessly in this barren place? The general is lost and will not admit it. Why else would we pass these stony hills twice in one day?"

Huo-hsin looked up at the hills. "I thought they looked familiar! With this wind blowing sand in our faces all day, I doubt anyone else has noticed. I will speak with the captain."

After the captain listened to Huo-hsin's concern about the general and their predicament, he paused. He knew Huo-hsin never jumped to conclusions. Finally he spoke: "Night is falling. We will camp in the shelter of this hill and see what the morning brings."

In the morning, the soldiers were surprised to find the general gone, and they grew angry when they realized that they had been deceived: He had gotten them lost on purpose and then returned to the army from Ku-Chu. He had never switched his loyalty to the army of Chi!

"Kao Ma!" Huo-hsin cried. "We are lost! We will surely die of thirst!"

Kao Ma tossed his head. "Lost? You men might be lost, but I am not! Tell the captain to let the horses lead and we will find the way home."

And so it was that Kao Ma led the army of Chi out of the desert, just in time to greet a very surprised General Huang-hua and the invaders from Ku-Chu, who were pushed back into their own lands, never again to challenge the men and horses of Chi.

1907 · 1919 · 1931
1943 · 1955 · 1967
1979 · 1991 · 2003

羊 The Year of the Sheep

The Year of the Sheep (sometimes called the Year of the Ram) is a time of peace and contentment. The frantic activity of the previous year, the Year of the Horse, gives way to a slower pace. People are calmer, with more time to be caring toward their family and friends. It's a perfect time for a nice, relaxing vacation.

A person born in the Year of the Sheep . . .
- Is shy, gentle, and soft-spoken, and dislikes arguments of all kinds.
- Values beauty and has good taste.
- Is involved in the arts—music, theater, painting, poetry.
- Is a true healer and would make a wonderful doctor, nurse, or other professional who cares for the sick.
- Never criticizes and is liked by all.

But Sheep can have trouble if . . .
- His quiet nature is mistaken for weakness.
- His good taste and love of beauty become a bit too expensive.

Friends and Others . . .
- Sheep might not get along with: Rat, Ox, or Dog
- Sheep's best companions: All others—but Boar, Rabbit, and Horse are at the top of the list

The Lost Lamb

Long ago a farmer discovered that one of his young sheep was missing. He quickly called to all his servants and everyone in his family, and, spreading out to cover every possible direction, they began to look for the lamb.

Now, the farmer's neighbor happened to be the old philosopher Yang-tse. When Yang-tse saw all the commotion outside his house, he asked his neighbor what the trouble was and the farmer told the old man of his missing lamb.

Yang-tse then asked, "Why do you send so many people to search for one lamb?"

The answer to this question seemed obvious to the farmer. "As you can see, there are many roads leading from our barn. We don't know which one the lamb may have followed, so each of us takes a different path to look for the little fellow."

Yang-tse was a good neighbor and volunteered the help of his servants and some of his disciples. Nonetheless, as the sun was setting, each man returned, exhausted, and informed Yang-tse that he had not found the wayward lamb.

The old philosopher was astounded. "Half the village was out all day looking for this foolish lamb and still no one saw him?"

The eldest servant replied, "Not only are there many roads leading away from here, but each of those has more roads branching from it! Never mind finding one errant lamb—it's a wonder we found our way home! I'm going to bed."

Yang-tse appeared to be quite disturbed by this news and fell into silent contemplation for a very long time. His worried disciples finally roused him. "Master, it is, after all, only a single lamb, and it's not even yours! Why are you so worried about him?"

Yang-tse heaved a great sigh, "It's not the lamb that concerns me, but rather all the branches in the road that led him astray! We too can be easily distracted and led away from those things that are important to us! In our wandering we can end up being just as lost as that silly lamb! We must hope that in remembering the love and good care he received at our neighbor's, he will be able to find his way to the farmer who is still out looking for him."

Sure enough, at dawn the following day, as Yang-tse and his disciples watched, the farmer trudged along on the road toward his home, with the lamb following close behind.

1908·1920·1932
1944·1956·1968
1980·1992·2004

猴 The Year of the Monkey

The Year of the Monkey is a time for courage, action, and success.

The monkey has been loved and celebrated throughout Chinese history as a fearless hero and a quick-witted trickster. There are countless stories of her cleverness—some telling of times when Monkey is too clever for her own good!

A person born in the Year of the Monkey . . .

- Is a clever free spirit with plenty of physical stamina.
- Is a born leader who is trusted by all those around her.
- Is skilled at working with her hands—doing needlework or carpentry, or fixing anything mechanical, such as a bike or car.
- Is generous and helpful.

But Monkey can have trouble if . . .

- Someone tries to tell her what to do. She can lead—but it's harder for her to follow!
- She has to finish a job. Her playful nature can get in the way and her quick mind means she's easily bored—which mean that Monkey sometimes drifts away from her work.

Friends and Others . . .

- Monkey might not get along with: Tiger (a bit too bossy and Monkey's exact opposite)
- Monkey's best companions: Rat (they both love making money!) and Dragon

24

The Monkeys and the Chestnuts

In days gone by there lived a man named Tzu-kung who loved all animals but held a special place in his heart for monkeys. In his spacious garden there lived a great many monkeys, and he attended to their every need. Over time he came to understand them and their ways so well that he could speak to them—and because monkeys are very intelligent, it wasn't long before they were able to understand his words.

In time it so happened that Tzu-kung's business began suffering financial trouble, and it became difficult for him to feed all of the monkeys in his garden. He soon realized that he had no choice but to cut back on the food he gave them each day, leaving them to find food for themselves, as most monkeys do. Now, Tzu-kung's monkeys loved him very much in return for all his kindness . . . but monkeys can be bad-tempered when things don't go their way.

One day, as Tzu-kung was grimly reviewing the receipts for his business, he said to himself, *"If I explain the situation to them, they will understand that it is a temporary setback . . . and surely they will not be too upset."*

So he gathered all the monkeys together and explained: "Until business picks up again, I can no longer give each of you four chestnuts in the morning and four in the evening. I shall have to give you each *three* chestnuts in the morning and four in the evening."

The monkeys, of course, were not happy to hear this. They screeched and bared their teeth, jumped up and down, thrashed the ground with branches, and generally carried on like very spoiled monkeys. Tzu-kung took a deep breath and tried to calm them down before they completely disrupted his lovely garden. Then an idea came to him. "I have a suggestion!" he called out above the din. "I will INCREASE the size of your breakfast to four chestnuts in the morning and give you three chestnuts in the evening!"

The monkeys, upon hearing that their breakfast of chestnuts would increase, gleefully swung from branch to branch and thumped their chests with pride in their victory. Monkeys are smart, but on that day Tzu-kung was smarter—and peace and contentment once again prevailed in his garden.

1909·1921·1933
1945·1957·1969
1981·1993·2005

鶏 The Year of the Rooster

The Year of the Rooster is a time to be practical. Hard work and discipline in this year will bring success.

In Chinese mythology the rooster is often depicted perched on a large drum once used to call troops to battle. But as one legend tells, during the reign of Emperor Yao, the land was free from war for so long that chickens nested in the unused drum. Since that time the drum and rooster have become symbols of peace.

A person born in the Year of the Rooster . . .

- Is a hardworking perfectionist who pays attention to every detail in his work.
- Has a sharp mind, which helps him to figure out what needs to be done and then to do it.
- Always follows the rules.

But Rooster can have trouble if . . .

- He gets a little too proud of his hard work—and expects other people to notice it and praise him again and again.
- He tries too hard to stand out from the crowd—and is a little too sure he's always right.

Friends and Others . . .

- Rooster might not get along with: Rabbit
- Rooster's best companions: Dragon is tops, but Ox and Snake also harmonize with him

Why Rooster Crows

The Emperor of Heaven was so busy that he could not find the time to look after all the things that required his attention. The rain, for example, simply fell wherever it wished to, so that one part of the world had drought while another endured floods. The result was a constant stream of prayers from the people on earth who suffered—so many prayers that he could never answer them all. So the emperor decided to appoint a God of Rain to make sure that everyone on earth received exactly what was needed. Any animal who might be interested in being God of Rain was to make an appointment to meet with him.

But the emperor found none of them suitable. Fox was too sly, Tiger was too powerful, Elephant was too clumsy, and Snake was too cunning.

When Dragon heard that the emperor had rejected such qualified animals, he decided he wouldn't even bother asking for the job. He said glumly to his friend, Rooster, "Though I can breathe fire, I am not fierce enough to be a god. But you—you have such wonderful feathers and such magnificent horns!"

Rooster shook his head. "I do not want to be God of Rain. I'm already king of the barnyard . . . but I've got an idea! I'll lend you my horns! You'll look so impressive that I'm sure the emperor will offer you the job!" Then generous Rooster unscrewed the horns from his head and handed them to his friend.

It so happened that Dragon impressed the emperor a great deal and became the new God of Rain. He thanked Rooster profusely for lending him his horns and then quite carefully asked, "May I keep them just a little longer—until I am used to the job?" Reluctantly, Rooster agreed.

Soon Dragon was so busy trying to control the rain that his friend rarely saw him. But Rooster missed his horns a great deal, and so, each morning as the sun rose, he called to Dragon, hoping his friend would hear him before he began his daily tasks. "Cock-a-doodle-doo!" Rooster called to get Dragon's attention.

And each day Dragon replied, "I know, Rooster, I know! I'll return them as soon as I teach the rain to do what I tell it! Ask me again tomorrow!"

Of course, Dragon still cannot control the rain—and so, of course, Rooster still calls to him every morning, hoping to get back his horns.

1910 · 1922 · 1934
1946 · 1958 · 1970
1982 · 1994 · 2006

狗 *The Year of the Dog*

The Year of the Dog is a time of honesty and fairness. All sides of a question or problem are considered very carefully so that the solution is sure to be fair.

A person born in the Year of the Dog . . .

- Is loyal and trustworthy—she stands by her friends through thick and thin.
- Will give up anything for something she believes is right.
- Is honest as can be. Dog always tells the truth!
- Is a great teammate or partner and works well with rules—whether playing a sport, singing in a choir, or working at school.

But Dog can have trouble if . . .

- She lets her emotions get the better of her—her temper can be red-hot!
- Her strong feelings make it hard for her to see that some things in life aren't completely good or completely bad, exactly right or exactly wrong. Some things in life are in between.

Friends and Others . . .

- Dog might not get along with: Dragon—who is everything she doesn't trust
- Dog's best companions: Tiger is a perfect match and Horse is a true friend

28

The Good Dog Fireball

The people who lived in the Land of Darkness were tired of bumping into things, bruising knees and banging noses. It was time they had some light. They weren't greedy, however; like the people down on earth, they would be perfectly content with light for just half the day. So they appealed to the king to help them.

The king said to his people, "Yes, some light would be nice—Ouch! I've just barked my shin on that darned throne!" And just then an idea occurred to him. "*Barked!* Of course! Bring me my faithful dog, Fireball."

Then the king explained his plan to the people gathered before him (though it was too dark to actually see if they were still there): "We can borrow the sun from the people down on earth when they are sleeping! Fireball, the bravest and most loyal dog in all the Land of Darkness, fetch the sun for us!"

So Fireball was sent to bring the sun to the Land of Darkness. Though the trip from her home to the skies of the earth was long and tiring, Fireball did as her master bade her. When she finally reached the sun, she opened her great mouth, bit into it—and then spat it right out again, howling, "Yow! That's HOT!" And with that, she tucked her tail between her legs and ran straight back to the Land of Darkness and her bowl of water.

When the dog explained his problem, the king understood and so asked Fireball to fetch the moon instead. After all, a little bit of light in the Land of Darkness was better than none at all. But when Fireball reached the moon, it was so cold that it nearly froze her tongue before she could spit it out. She returned to her home once more, but the king would not give up on his faithful friend: "Carry this water with you and try again to fetch the sun." When this second effort did not work, the king sent Fireball back to the moon, this time with a blanket to first warm it. Fireball still had no luck, but the king refused to stop trying. Back and forth Fireball traveled, to the moon, then to the sun, again and again.

And despite being tired, Fireball hasn't given up yet, for every time we on earth see an eclipse of the sun or the moon, that's the king's faithful dog closing her great mouth around it for just a moment or two in her eternal quest to bring light to the Land of Darkness.

1911 · 1923 · 1935
1947 · 1959 · 1971
1983 · 1995 · 2007

豕者 The Year of the Boar

The Year of the Boar (also called the Year of the Pig) is a time of peace, friendship, and harmony. It's too much hard work to compete for power and glory all the time! The Boar's motto: Enjoy your friendships and have a little fun!

A person born in the Year of the Boar . . .

- Is intelligent.
- Is good-natured, kind, and very generous.
- Makes friends easily—and knows how to be a good friend.
- Loves *everything* that's beautiful (such as a new, bright gold watch), or delicious (such as a triple chocolate fudge ice-cream sundae), or especially soft and warm to the touch (such as a thick, flannel comforter on a cold winter night).
- Is an optimist—Boar believes that great things can happen and that deep down, all people are good, not evil.

But Boar can have trouble if . . .

- Someone who is more nasty than nice decides to take advantage of her kindness.
- She spends all her money on the things she loves—which is everything that's beautiful, delicious, or soft and warm.
- She gets angry. (It's hard to make Boar angry, but once she's mad—watch out!)

Friends and Others . . .

- Boar might not get along with: Snake—their ideas are often exact opposites
- Boar's best companions: Everyone else, especially Sheep and Rabbit

30

The Clever Pig

There once was a wealthy farmer named Li Tai-yeh, or Big Master Li. He was a kind man who was generous with his riches to all those around him.

Li Tai-yeh also took very good care of his animals, feeding them well, giving them warm homes, and asking nothing in return. But the animals were honorable and took it upon themselves to assist Li Tai-yeh. Dog was the watchman, Rooster awakened everyone for work each morning, and Cat kept the farm free of mice and rats. Horse pulled the farmer's wagon, Ox plowed the rice paddies, and Donkey carried Li Tai-yeh's son to school and back every day. Everyone returned the farmer's kindness as best he or she could and was happy to do so. Everyone, that is, except Pig.

She believed she was too smart to work for her supper. The other animals suggested that she stand up and do something useful, but Pig replied with a lazy grunt, "The farmer feeds me all I can eat, whether I do any work or not. Why on earth would I want to get to work in the morning when I could be sleeping soundly in my pen? And in the afternoon I have to nap after my lunch—how can I be expected to work then? As for the night, no one works at night, except Cat! Please don't bother me with such nonsense!" Then, with a disdainful snort, she rolled over and went back to sleep.

Not only did Pig refuse to work, she ate everything in sight, then complained that she hadn't been given enough! In fact, she did nothing but eat, sleep, complain, and say to herself, "What a clever pig I am! I eat all I want and I don't have to lift a hoof for it!" Thus it wasn't long before she became the fattest pig in the province.

One day, Li Tai-yeh's neighbor Chiang saw huge Pig wallowing in the mud and said to Li Tai-yeh, "This hog is eating you out of house and home and does nothing for you! I'll trade you my flock of ducks for her. At least they'll lay some eggs for you."

So the deal was struck. Chiang trussed up Pig and carted her off to market. Pig squealed like a pig the whole way and was never seen or heard from again.

The other animals just shook their heads and said, *"Tsung-ming pei tsung-ming wu,"* which means, "Smart people often defeat themselves with their own cleverness!"

Acknowledgments

I wish to thank everyone at Inner Traditions, but especially Jon Graham, Jeanie Levitan, Elaine Sanborn, and Ehud Sperling for making this book possible. I also want to acknowledge the assistance of John Brook Lalley, and Amy Grasmick and Judith Flint of the Kimball Library in Randolph, Vermont. An invaluable resource was found in *Taoist Astrology: A Handbook of the Authentic Chinese Tradition* by Susan Levitt with Jean Tang, published by Destiny Books. The stories in this book were inspired by or adapted from folk tales collected by Ruth Q. Sun in her book, *The Asian Animal Zodiac,* published by Castle Books.

About the Author

Gregory Crawford's career as an artist began when he was still in high school. His work has appeared in books and magazines, and on buildings, T-shirts, television, and the Internet. He also loves to give watercolor paintings to his friends.

Greg cannot remember a time when he was not fascinated by Chinese culture, especially the beautiful simplicity of the paintings of Xia Chang. In fact, he believes he may have been Chinese in a past life.

The pictures in this book have been done in mixed media: pen and ink, watercolor, gouache, acrylics, and colored pencil. Never a purist, Greg has been known to use coffee to achieve just the color he wanted.

Greg lives in central Vermont with his wife, Jacki, their German shepherd, Athena, a grumpy cat, and a noisy cockatiel named Beethoven.